My Protest

CITY HALL

By: Linda Gaston-Bessellieu
Co-Authors: Tawana Bessellieu & Jaliyah Bessellieu-Webb
Illustrations By: Juanita Taylor

Foreword

Being brave and taking a stand are wonderful lessons and we must embrace these characteristics of strength at an early age.

In this story, the main character learns how to take a stand for what is right. Read this book and never stop standing for justice.

-Angela Bivins author of
The Survivor's Chronicles: The chronicles of Angela the Brave

My Protest is life-changing. I was so excited to share this real-life inspired story with young readers and writers. As an educator, I am always looking for new material to share with my students. This awesome tale allows the reader to make connections to real-life situations and it provides an example of how people of all ages can come together to make a positive difference in our society.

As the director of the young writer's program at my elementary school, I was able to invite the very talented and up-and-coming young author Jaliyah Bessellieu to speak with the students in the group about the writing process. She was poised and confidently shared with the group of students in the young writer's club about the entire process of conceptualizing an idea and taking it to an amazing level of completion. She answered every question like a rock star.

This text would be a great resource for students to learn about standing for justice and doing something brave. This story gets the Angela Apple Stamp of Approval.

-Ms. Angela Bivins- educator and author of
The Survivor's Chronicles: The chronicles of Angela the Brave

READERS' FAVORITE
5 STAR REVIEWS

"Told through the eyes of four-a-half-year-old Jaliyah. The experience is further underscored by the prevalence of the worldwide COVID-19 pandemic, as Jaliyah describes what she saw, heard, and felt when she joined family members in one of the many powerful Black Lives Matter marches."
Jamie Michele

"I thought My Protest was an amazing book that discussed a very serious movement in a way that a child audience could understand."
Tiffany Ferrell

"For those who feel threatened by such demonstrations, this children's book should be a real eye-opener, with it serving to dispel many myths and fears related to such socio-political activity."
Lois Henderson

"Young children often see and hear more than we think, so it is so important to have a book like My Protest, which can be used to help them understand the world around them."
Kristine Zimmerman

"The story portrays the message against racism clearly, in a way that a child can easily understand. With cute and colorful illustrations, My Protest captures the attention of its readers while its message appeals to their hearts."
Cassie Widjaja

To order additional copies of this book, contact:
Xlibris
844-714-8691
www.Xlibris.com
Orders@Xlibris.com

ISBN: 978-1-6641-2820-0 (sc)
ISBN: 978-1-6641-2819-4 (e)

Print information available on the last page

Rev. date: 09/28/2022

MY PROTEST

BY: LINDA GASTON-BESSELLIEU

CO-AUTHORS:
TAWANA BESSELLIEU
& JALIYAH BESSELLIEU-WEBB

Dedication

In loving memory of GiGi.,
(Virgie) and my Dad (Laricus).

To my family

"If you set your goals ridiculously high, and it's a failure, you will fail above everyone else's success."
                                    – James Cameron

Special thanks to my sister-in-law for inviting us to the protest.

Special thanks to Rev. H. Jenkins for your many prayers.

INTRODUCTION

This nonfiction story is told from the perception of a 4-year-old child. She attended a peaceful Black Lives Matter protest along with her mother, aunt, and cousin at the height of the pandemic and the George Floyd incident. My Protest is a book that teachers and parents will appreciate having as a resource.

Today, I went to a protest with my mom, aunt, and cousin, Camille. Other children were there with their parents.

A protest is walking, and people are saying things, so black men, children, and women won't get killed.

My cousin and I had to wear a mask to cover our nose and mouth so we wouldn't get Coronavirus. Everyone wore a mask. The virus can make you sick, it can kill people, and you can't touch things. You can't go outside to play with your friends.

The leader was in the front
of the line. She said, "We
are here to protest and stay
with your family."

The leader told us to walk and say, "No justice, no peace! No racists, police!" Sometimes we had to say, "Black lives matter!" and hold up our fist.

We walked around, holding up our signs and sometimes our fist. My mommy helped me make my poster at home. My poster said, "My Life Matters!" My Cousin, Camille, and the other children had signs too.

People came by in their cars looking. They were honking the horn. The police rode by and looked at us.

Some People took pictures of us. A nice man asked us if we wanted water, and a lady asked us if we need a ride to our car. My aunt said, "No, thank you."

Protesting was a lot of fun, but I was tired. My cousin, Camille, was tired too. My mom and aunt took us home.

Jaliyah and her mother
at the protest.

Printed in the United States
by Baker & Taylor Publisher Services